Contents

D0345742

WOULD YOU RATHER RANDOMS: A collection of hilarious hypothetical questions

- By Clint Hammerstrike

To my amazing wife Emma who has spent the last 10 years enduring my favourite pastime of asking ridiculous "would you rather questions". You are my rock, my love and my hypothetical comedy companion!

About the Author

Someone with plenty of free time to write this book and enough imagination to make up the name Clint Hammerstrike. Seriously why wouldn't you?

What else is there to say other than you will be pleased to know this isn't my day job!

Introduction

Writing this book has been one of the simplest things that I have ever done (I live a very complicated life – kind of a big deal)! This is because I have spent a lifetime pondering random scenarios and questions. If I had a pound for every time I had contemplated the questions would I rather X OR Y, I would be richer than Scrooge McDuck - but I would rather be poor and be Mickey Mouse.

I wrote this book to share with you some of the great conundrums we face as humanity such as: Would you rather brush your teeth with a rat OR a Pigeon? Would you rather have all your meals covered in gravy OR cheese for a year? Would you rather carry hot soup in your hands OR a lobster in your underwear? This book will also help you sort your wreck of a life out by exploring important life scenarios such as:

- What you would do if trapped in an underground shelter for three years?
- What would be the soundtrack to your life?
- How would you survive a Zombie Koala attack?

Remember all of these scenarios are for hypothetical entertainment purposes and should not be taken as a recommendation or an endorsement. You should never lick a toilet (no matter it's state of cleanliness), kick your partners mother in the shins, or use an old-age pensioner as a weapon to fight off Zombie Koalas. Did I really need to say that last sentence!?!

Helpful Guide

To aid you on this journey of self-discovery I have suggested a couple of rules to help you through.

Rule 1: You must answer. Even if you would rather do neither you MUST pick!

Rule 2: Don't rush your answer. Give yourself time to consider the sheer complexity and horror of the choice!

Rule 3: Respect the opinion of those reading with you? Even when they are plainly wrong!

Rule 4: Take this seriously, we are considering the meaning of life do not even consider laughing!

Rule 5: Forget rule 4. Laugh, come on its sucking on a marathon runners sock OR licking a goats face. Enough said!

Chapter one: Nice and Simple

WOULD YOU RATHER:

Have a hairy nose OR hairy ears?

WOULD YOU RATHER:

Always have a runny nose OR a cough?

WOULD YOU RATHER:

Make the sound of a cat OR a dog when you fart?

WOULD YOU RATHER:

Bite your tongue OR stub your toe?

WOULD YOU RATHER:

Constantly smell really bad but not be able to smell yourself (everyone else can) OR be constantly surrounded by an awful stench that you can smell (but you don't smell)?

WOULD YOU RATHER:

Brush your teeth with a rat OR a pigeon?

WOULD YOU RATHER:

Cry cola OR chocolate milk tears?

WOULD YOU RATHER:

Always be hungry OR thirsty?

WOULD YOU RATHER:

Suck on a marathon runners sock OR lick a goat's face?

WOULD YOU RATHER:

Eat the contents of a spot OR a blister?

WOULD YOU RATHER:

Only be able to eat food that was too spicy OR too salty?

WOULD YOU RATHER:

Be able to make people cry OR laugh by touching them?

WOULD YOU RATHER:

Be a vampire OR a werewolf?

WOULD YOU RATHER:

Be able to read people's minds OR control people's minds?

WOULD YOU RATHER:

Have £1million pounds that you could only spend on other people OR £20,000 that you could only spend on yourself?

WOULD YOU RATHER:

Have a Ferrari and not be able to drive it OR a Vauxhall Corsa and be able to drive it?

WOULD YOU RATHER:

Sleep without a pillow OR a duvet?

WOULD YOU RATHER:

Catch a hedgehog OR a skunk falling from a tower block?

WOULD YOU RATHER:

Be trapped in a lift with a couple kissing OR fighting?

WOULD YOU RATHER:

Climb to the top of Everest OR win an Olympic Gold Medal?

WOULD YOU RATHER:

Never have to shower again OR never have to change your clothes again?

WOULD YOU RATHER:

Live in the White House OR Buckingham Palace?

WOULD YOU RATHER:

Be able to breakdance OR rap?

You are really hungry after another kale smoothie cleanse. Luckily for you a new restaurant has opened up in town. You are invited out by friends to try the new tasting menu where you get to pick each course. Calories don't count so let yourself go. What would you choose:

- First Starter?

- Second Starter?

- First Main?

- Second Main?

- Third Main?

- First Dessert?

- Second Dessert?

- Third Dessert?

- Drink Number 1?

- Drink Number 2?

You go out for a walk one day and fall off a cliff. Thankfully science can rebuild you, but not as you once were. Using ground breaking technology scientist can mix animal body parts together to give you a new body. Luckily you can pick which animal for each part. What do you choose:

- Toes?

- Feet?

- Legs?

- Torso?

- Fingers?

- Arms?

- Neck?

- Face?

- Hair?

- Voice?

Life is hard and you deserve a holiday. But who can be bothered to go to the effort of booking a holiday. Isn't it much easier to just hand your credit card and pin number over to a strange man with a globe and a trench coat and let him plan it for you. Kindly he has provided a couple of options for you to choose from. If you're going to make your friends jealous on Facebook and Instagram, you better choose wisely. So would you rather go on holiday to:

- A Russian military prison OR a donkey waxing camp?

- A silent retreat OR a theme park?

- A relaxing beach holiday OR a skiing trip?

- A tropical jungle adventure OR a snowy mountain expedition?

- Inner city Birmingham OR Slough?

- Inter-railing through Europe OR backpacking across Australia?
- A steam train convention in Basingstoke OR an intensive cross-stitch course in Stoke?

- Clubbing in Ibiza OR sightseeing in Venice?

- New York OR Johannesburg?

- A monkey OR a polar bear sanctuary?

It is Sunday evening and you are hungry. As you scavenge through the cupboards and fridge you curse the fact that your online groceries aren't being delivered until tomorrow. Looks like you are going to have to come up with some creative combinations. So would you rather eat:

- Tuna and marmite OR cheese and gravy?

- Jam and kale OR cornflakes and mayonnaise?

- A lemon and instant noodles OR tomato sauce and banana?

- Bread and jelly OR pasta and chocolate sauce?

- Spinach and honey OR satsuma and pickle?

- Cucumber and Pop Tarts OR tomato soup and porridge?

- Egg and peanut butter OR tofu and bacon?

- Curry paste and strawberries OR ice cream and rice?

- Cream cheese and chocolate spread OR mushrooms and popcorn?

- Potato and Haribo OR couscous and marshmallow fluff?

Chapter Two: Slightly harder

WOULD YOU RATHER:

Always be too hot OR too cold?

WOULD YOU RATHER:

Have the neck of a giraffe OR the flippers of a penguin?

WOULD YOU RATHER:

Never have to poo OR be sick again?

WOULD YOU RATHER:

Have eyes on your elbows OR a mouth on your stomach?

WOULD YOU RATHER:

Have no eyes but still be able to see OR no nose and still be able to smell?

WOULD YOU RATHER:

Have an itch that you can't scratch OR a sneeze that won't come out?

WOULD YOU RATHER:

Sneeze out of your bottom OR fart out of your mouth?

WOULD YOU RATHER:

Have a toe for a tongue OR tongues for toes?

WOULD YOU RATHER:

Have all your meals for a year covered in cheese OR gravy?

WOULD YOU RATHER:

Eat a hotdog with chocolate sauce on it OR an ice cream with ketchup on it?

WOULD YOU RATHER:

Eat 10 caterpillars OR have to wear them as a necklace for a day?

WOULD YOU RATHER:

Only eat stuffing for the rest of your life OR only drink gravy for the rest of your life?

WOULD YOU RATHER:

Eat a puppy that tastes like chocolate OR a kitten that tastes like strawberries?

WOULD YOU RATHER:

Be the fastest person in the world OR the strongest?

WOULD YOU RATHER:

Be able to stop time OR travel back in time?

WOULD YOU RATHER:

Only be able to communicate by singing OR whispering in people's ears?

WOULD YOU RATHER:

Have to carry hot soup in your hands OR a lobster in your underwear?

WOULD YOU RATHER:

Wear wet socks for a day OR an itchy woollen jumper?

WOULD YOU RATHER:

Wear someone else's used underwear OR use someone else's toothbrush?

WOULD YOU RATHER:

Always have to answer truthfully OR always lie?

WOULD YOU RATHER:

Fight off a dog sized rat OR a cow sized ant?

WOULD YOU RATHER:

Lie in a bath of spiders OR snakes?

WOULD YOU RATHER:

Remember everything (and not be able to forget) OR be able to completely forget anything?

WOULD YOU RATHER:

Have to speak everything on your mind OR never be able to speak again?

WOULD YOU RATHER:

Know how you're going to die OR when you're going to die?

WOULD YOU RATHER:

Be the cleverest person in a room OR the funniest?

Rocky, The Sound of Music and Top Gun what do they all have in common other than being adrenaline junkie movies? That's right a killer soundtrack. So why should you have to walk around like an extra rather than a movie star. It's time to give your life a re-make! What song would you rather hear rising from the background at these key moments:

- Being born?

- Growing up?

- First Kiss?

- Graduation?

- First Job?

- Wedding?

- First Child?

- Middle Age?

- Growing Old?

- Death Scene?

You have been training for this for weeks, doing sit-ups, playing old school Tekken and eating Beef Jerky. You find yourself in the ring and the crowd are cheering. You are ready to fight, now you just have to select your opponent. So would you rather fight:

- Peppa Pig OR Tinky Winky?

- A lion sized koala OR a koala sized lion?

- Seventy, five year olds OR five, seventy year olds?

- Your mum OR your partner?

- A granny OR a puppy?

- A politician OR a banker?

- A dentist OR a traffic warden?

- A Dachshund sized T-Rex OR a T-Rex sized Dachshund?

- Thor OR The Hulk?

- A heavyweight boxer OR a Sumo Wrestler?

Money is tight and you have to find a way to pay the bills. Medical experimentation is the way to go – Am I right??? You sign up at the clinic and change into a gown that doesn't hide your backside (what's the deal with that?). A doctor hands you a clipboard for you to select the trials you would like to take part in. Picking the wrong one could have some uncomfortable side effects. So would you rather side effects that:

- Make you talk in Taylor Swift Lyrics OR Yoda quotes?

- Make you see in black and white OR hear everyone speaking like Ned Flanders?

- Make your urine rainbow coloured OR smell like strawberries?

- Make you punch yourself every time you blink OR kick yourself every fifth breath you take?

- Make you sound like Darth Vader OR Elmo?

- Make you irresistible to Camels OR Llamas?

- Make you able to break dance OR speak another language?

- Change your hands to pizza wheels OR sparklers?

- Give you cravings for sand OR dry skin flakes?

- Make you cry when you should laugh OR laugh when you should cry?

Regrets? Self-loathing? Asking yourself what am I doing with my life (issues I have asked myself writing this book)! Wouldn't it be easier if I could just start all over again? Wouldn't it be better if you were a part time Barista/full time sky diver? Who says a leopard can't change its spots? It's time to sort out your life. So would you rather:

- Stop world hunger OR find a cure for cancer?

- Bring an end to all wars OR end global poverty?

- Adopt a litter of kittens OR a litter of puppies?

- Be a spy OR a doctor?

- Be a poet OR a mime artist?

- Own a bakery OR a sweet shop?

- Be the president of the USA OR Queen/King of England?

- Have a number one hit song OR number one box office movie?

- Be a painter OR an author?

- Save the earth from a meteor OR an alien invasion?

Chapter Three: Hmm that's tricky

WOULD YOU RATHER:

Have Pool balls for eyes OR Dominoes for teeth?

WOULD YOU RATHER:

Sweat melted cheese OR chocolate sauce?

WOULD YOU RATHER:

Have a head twice as small OR twice as big?

WOULD YOU RATHER:

Have the ears of a bunny OR the tail of a horse?

WOULD YOU RATHER:

Have the fur of a bear OR the feathers of a flamingo?

WOULD YOU RATHER:

Eat through your bottom OR poo through your mouth?

WOULD YOU RATHER:

Use eye drops made of chilli sauce OR toilet paper made of sandpaper?

WOULD YOU RATHER:

Eat your toe OR your finger?

WOULD YOU RATHER:

Drink lemonade through your nose OR your eyes?

WOULD YOU RATHER:

Be fed spoon-fed dinner by Dracula OR Voldemort?

WOULD YOU RATHER:

Have all sweet food taste savoury OR all savoury food taste sweet?

WOULD YOU RATHER:

Eat food that has been pre-chewed by a stranger OR a dog?

WOULD YOU RATHER:

Be able to drink lava OR eat metal?

WOULD YOU RATHER:

Be able to run super-fast OR slow time down?

WOULD YOU RATHER:

Be able to swim like a shark OR run like a cheetah?

WOULD YOU RATHER:

No one turns up for your wedding OR your funeral?

WOULD YOU RATHER:

Be able to speak every language OR communicate with animals?

WOULD YOU RATHER:

Always get away with lying OR always know when someone is lying to you?

WOULD YOU RATHER:

Speak every language OR play every musical instrument?

WOULD YOU RATHER:

Be trapped in space OR at the bottom of the ocean?

WOULD YOU RATHER:

Always have a terrible song stuck in your head OR have the same nightmare each night?

WOULD YOU RATHER:

Raise sheep for eggs OR chickens for wool?

WOULD YOU RATHER:

Be the best player on a losing team OR the worst player on a winning team?

WOULD YOU RATHER:

Stand up and sing in-front of a group of work colleagues OR strangers?

WOULD YOU RATHER:

Not be able to access the internet OR not see anyone for a month?

Your new kitchen has been installed and you are ready to get your apron on and create a gastronomic marvel. But you can't keep this decadent feast to yourself you need some dinner guests. The question is who should you invite? You flick through your endless contacts list but who would you rather invite from these categories:

- A sport person?

- A film star?

- A musician?

- A dead person from history (not decomposed and fit for the dinner table)?

- A family Member?

- A friend?

- A cartoon character?

- A superhero?

- A fictional character?

- One freebie choice?

The cruise ship captain has taken a wrong turn somewhere off the Island of Fiji. You are now shipwrecked with little chance of survival! Fortunately, you have been marooned with a diverse range of people. The island is only big enough to support 11 people. Guess it's time to start choosing your survival crew. Your survival will depend on them. So, who would you rather?

- Antony McPartlin OR Declan Donnelly?

- Arnold Schwarzenegger OR Sylvester Stallone?

- James Bond OR Jason Bourne?

- Homer Simpson OR Peter Griffin?

- Donald Trump OR Vladimir Putin?

- Katniss Everdeen OR Rey?

- Cast of Friends: Chandler, Joey, Monica, Phoebe, Rachel, Ross (choose one)?

- Jon Snow OR Daenerys Targaryen?

- Ironman OR Captain America?

- Pooh Bear OR Tigger?

- Doctor Who OR Sherlock Holmes?

On a lovely day trip out you fall into a nuclear reactor. Somehow you survive the brutal gamma rays. As you clench tight trying to avoid becoming a green rage filled beast you face the choice of what superpowers you will take on. Remember with great power comes great responsibility! So, would you rather:

- Be a superhero OR a supervillain?

- Be invisible OR able to fly?

- Age at half the speed OR run 100 times the speed of a normal human?

- Be able to lift up lorries with your hands OR with your mind?

- Be able to create fire OR ice?

- Be able to stretch to incredible lengths OR shrink to microscopic size?

- Have x-ray vision OR supersonic hearing?

- Be able to shoot lasers out of your eyes OR spider webs from your hands?

- Be able to move things with your mind OR control people's minds?

- Be super strong OR super smart?

You are walking down the street. As you enter the door of your local convenience store you are sucked into a Freaky Friday/13 again Vortex where you inhabit the body of a random person. Fortunately for you, you have some choice as to whose body that is. Pick well or suffer. So, would you rather be:

- Donald Trump OR a knife throwers assistant?

- A naked jellyfish handler OR a scorpion juggler?

- Your mum OR your dad?

- You 10 years ago OR you 10 years in the future?

- King Kong OR Godzilla?

- A dentist that has to give the Hulk root canal OR the hygiene therapist that has to give the Hulk a colonic?

- The tallest person in the world OR the shortest?

- A cast member from "The Only Way is Essex" OR "Made in Chelsea"?

- A medical trial participant for a laxatives company OR the cleaner for a laxative trial company?

- A member of the Mafia OR the Yakuza?

Chapter Four: Oh gosh help me

WOULD YOU RATHER:

Have six fingers on each hand OR 8 toes on each foot?

WOULD YOU RATHER:

Wear a snowsuit in the Sahara Desert OR be naked at the North Pole?

WOULD YOU RATHER:

Get a paper cut OR bite your tongue?

WOULD YOU RATHER:

Have fingers as long as your arms OR arms as long as your fingers?

WOULD YOU RATHER:

Have toes OR fingers like curly fries?

WOULD YOU RATHER:

Poo yourself every time someone says your name OR wet yourself every time you cough?

WOULD YOU RATHER:

When you squeeze a spot a whole tub of cream cheese comes out OR a slug?

WOULD YOU RATHER:

Spend the rest of your life with Wotsit dust on your hands OR sand in-between your toes?

WOULD YOU RATHER:

Eat your favourite meal for the rest of your life OR never again?

WOULD YOU RATHER:

Give up chocolate OR alcohol?

WOULD YOU RATHER:

Eat a loaf of mouldy bread OR drink a pint of gone off milk?

WOULD YOU RATHER:

Lick a stranger's armpit OR eat their snot?

WOULD YOU RATHER:

Be able to fly like a bird OR swim like a shark?

WOULD YOU RATHER:

Everything you think becomes true OR be able to control people with a PlayStation controller?

WOULD YOU RATHER:

Be Superman OR Batman?

WOULD YOU RATHER:

Live where it is constantly winter OR summer?

WOULD YOU RATHER:

Spend the rest of your life on a plane OR a boat?

WOULD YOU RATHER:

Spend twenty years in prison and then be found innocent OR be put away for 15 years (be innocent) but be considered guilty forever?

WOULD YOU RATHER:

Never eat chocolate OR never use a smartphone?

WOULD YOU RATHER:

Be stung by a jellyfish OR give up social media for 6 months?

WOULD YOU RATHER:

Be allergic to carbohydrates OR the internet?

WOULD YOU RATHER:

Lose all your photos OR all your technology?

WOULD YOU RATHER:

Go back into the past to meet your ancestors OR forward into the future to meet your great-great-great-great grandchildren?

WOULD YOU RATHER:

Get rich working hard OR winning the lottery?

WOULD YOU RATHER:

Hear the good news first OR the bad news first?

He only went and pushed the red button with those tiny hands of his! Now you are going to be stuck in an underground emergency shelter on your own for the next three years whilst you sit out the worst of it. The only problem is that you didn't stock up very well. Still, in the last few minutes before you close the hatch you have time to make some last minute choices. Choose wisely it is going to be a rough few years. What would you rather have as your:

- One movie?

- One TV boxset?

- Three luxury toiletries?

- One luxury food item (in addition to basic rations)?

- One luxury drink (to supplement water)?

- One book?

- One album?

- One conversation with a famous person for 30 minutes to be used at any time?

- One pet?

- One personal item?

The uprising has taken place, and you have been appointed world leader! Taking your place on your plush new throne you are asked to pass verdict on the most pressing issues of dystopian society. The fate of the world depends on you. So would you rather:

- Save the chocolate OR doughnut production factory?

- Save the crisps OR biscuit production factory?

- Save the alcohol OR toilet paper production factory?

- Save the last remaining boxset of TV Show "Friends" OR "Big Bang Theory"?

- Save cats OR dogs from extinction?

- Have working toilets OR working televisions?

- Have clothes OR beds?

- Have music OR meat?

- Have everyone greet you by high five OR fist bump?

- Have everyone tattooed on their forehead with a skateboarding badger OR a breakdancing porcupine?

It's happened Zombie Koala's have risen and are slowly chomping their way through the human race. Every time a person is bitten they transform into a monstrously cute Zombie Koala. If you are going to make it through to safety you are going to have to choose wisely. So would you rather:

- Use a 5-year-old OR an old age pensioner as a weapon?

- Use puppies OR kittens as body armour?

- Use your mother OR your partner as a distraction to escape?

- Loot a toy store OR a beauty salon for supplies?

- Team up with a band of Morris dancers OR Bell ringers?

- Hideout in an overflowing public toilet OR a container ship filled with rotting fish?

- Save a class of children from a viciously cute koala attack OR leave them to their fate and find a shotgun with plenty of ammo?

- Drink water filtered through a stranger's pants OR your own used toilet paper?

- Eat a non-zombie Koala raw OR a Zombie Koala cooked?

- Be the last human alive for eternity OR give up and join the Zombie Koalas?

Life is stressful and you deserve a relaxing bath. You put in your bath bomb, light a candle and turn on some whale music. You leave the bath running whilst you finish your stamp collection. But those stamps are so entertaining that you lose track of time. Next thing you know a tidal wave is coming out of the bathroom. In a few minutes your house will be ruined but you have time to save some possessions. The question is would you rather save:

- Your clothes OR your TV?

- Your smartphone OR your pet?

- Your photos OR your love letters?

- Your bed OR your sofa?

- Your laptop OR your tablet?

- Your fridge OR your oven?

- Your books OR your DVDs?

- Your watch OR your camera?

- Your wallet or your car keys?

- Your games console OR wedding album?

Chapter Five: I Surrender

WOULD YOU RATHER:

Always be sticky OR itchy?

WOULD YOU RATHER:

Have explosive diarrhoea OR projectile vomit?

WOULD YOU RATHER:

Bathe in other people's sweat -but come out clean OR never shower again and be smelly?

WOULD YOU RATHER:

Poo yourself every day for a month but nobody know OR poo yourself once and everybody know?

WOULD YOU RATHER:

Not be able to clean your teeth OR your armpits for a year?

WOULD YOU RATHER:

Have a 10 inch "innie" bellybutton OR a 10 inch "outie" bellybutton?

WOULD YOU RATHER:

Eat your food with your feet OR blow your nose with your tongue?

WOULD YOU RATHER:

Drink bin juice OR eat a stranger's fingernail clippings?

WOULD YOU RATHER:

All your food has toenails in it OR hair?

WOULD YOU RATHER:

Be Spider-man OR Ant-man?

WOULD YOU RATHER:

Be stupid in a world of clever people OR be clever in a world of stupid people?

WOULD YOU RATHER:

Only be able to speak in song OR only say 100 words in a day?

WOULD YOU RATHER:

Be able to spit custard OR mayonnaise?

WOULD YOU RATHER:

Win £50,000 OR your friend wins £500,000?

WOULD YOU RATHER:

Have a dog with a human face OR a cat with human hands?

WOULD YOU RATHER:

Have to touch someone with your nose every time you talk to them OR give them a foot rub when the conversation ends?

WOULD YOU RATHER:

Be stuck behind a slow walker OR have a stone in your shoe?

WOULD YOU RATHER:

Have to wear a Bikini/Mankini all the time OR never change your underwear again?

WOULD YOU RATHER:

Never be allowed inside OR outside?

WOULD YOU RATHER:

Wear clown clothes OR clown make up for the rest of your life?

WOULD YOU RATHER:

Have a visible bogey on your nose OR food on your face?

WOULD YOU RATHER:

Lick a clean toilet OR a used shower floor?

WOULD YOU RATHER:

Accidentally show up at a party in fancy dress (no-one else is wearing a costume) OR audibly fart in a lift and everyone know it was you?

WOULD YOU RATHER:

Be able to pee silently OR never need a poo when visiting other people's houses?

WOULD YOU RATHER:

Look good in every photograph OR always smell good?

WOULD YOU RATHER:

Live in eternal darkness OR bright light?

WOULD YOU RATHER:

Be successful in business OR successful in love?

WOULD YOU RATHER:

Use a toothbrush previously used to scrub your bathroom floor OR a toothbrush used to clean a stranger's mouth?

After a long day of playing Pokémon Go and freestyle rap battling you are exhausted and just want to get back to your hotel and relax. Sadly, the budget hotel you booked has had some problems with the booking so looks like your sharing a room! Thankfully the receptionist is feeling generous so you get to pick your roommate. So, would you rather share a room with:

- Rats OR bats?

- Mosquitos OR wasps?

- Scorpions OR snakes?

- A grizzly bear OR lion?

- Your partner's parents OR an alligator?

- Donald Trump OR an elderly nudist?

- An out of tune violinist OR an overflowing toilet?

- Someone throwing up OR someone with diarrhoea?

- Someone with a contagious rash OR angry bull?

- Someone that keeps pinching you OR someone who keeps pulling your hair?

You are going on a date. It's a blind date that your friends have set up for you at a restaurant. You have dressed in your best outfit and feel ready to go, However, on a first date who knows what will happen! So, would you rather your date:

- Has breath like a decomposing badger OR spits when they talk?

- Eats nothing and watches you judgingly as you eat OR steals your food whilst you are in the toilet?

- Talks about nothing but the pros and cons of printer paper OR doesn't talk at all?

- Only refers to themselves in the third person OR shouts when they talk?

- Only talks about their ex OR talks about your future wedding?

- Never makes eye contact OR stares intensely?

- Sings children's theme songs under their breath OR mutters about chasing badgers?

- Takes a sip of your drink and leaves food floaters OR wet sneezes in your food?

- Spends the whole time on Facebook OR continuously goes to the toilet?

- Orders expensive champagne and caviar and then runs out of the restaurant without paying OR throws a bowl of steaming tomato soup into your lap?

You are round your partner's parents' house for Sunday lunch. You get a text from an anonymous number, it reads: "I have taken your (insert most important thing in your life) hostage. If you do not follow my instructions, you will never see it/them again." You must complete ten challenges or else! So as you sit down for lunch would you rather:

- Kick your partners mum in the shins under the table OR pour hot gravy in your lap?

- Loudly say that you are glad there is sweetcorn as you are currently constipated OR drink the whole jug of steaming gravy?

- Eat your dinner like an animal without knife and fork OR start a food fight?

- Take your top off and wave it above your head football fan style OR kiss your partners father?

- Tell everyone that you don't believe in toilet paper and would rather use your hand to wipe

OR that the roast dinner tastes worse than the food you ate in prison?

- Rub salt OR pepper into your eyes?

- Tell your partners mother that you hate their home OR that you hate orphans?

- Stand up and freestyle rap "8 Mile" style OR sing opera style?

- Swallow your knife OR fork?

- Smash a plate over your head OR pour custard over your partner?

Humans suck right with all the wars, bullying and lying. Well not on your watch! As self-appointed "Minister for Fairness" it's time to get planet earth sorted. So would you rather stop:

- Bullying OR littering?

- People spitting OR leaving chewing gum on seats?

- Animal cruelty OR ocean pollution?

- People smoking OR speeding?

- Anti-social behaviour OR online trolling?

- Spam emails OR PPI calls?

- The sale of drugs OR guns?

- Tall people standing in front of you at gigs OR people walking slowly in front of you?

- Chefs spitting in food OR people weeing in swimming pools?

- People lying OR stealing?

The big day has arrived. As you make your way to your job interview you are feeling confident and ready to impress. When you sit down though, things begin to change and you start to feel the first prickles of panic. In the words of Dr. Pepper what's the worst that can happen! Would you rather:

- Your CV turns out to be a naked picture of yourself OR the plans for a terrorist plot?

- Audibly poo yourself OR vomit when asked about your strengths?

- Give a presentation and mid-way through realise you are only wearing pants OR that you have been singing the lyrics to Miley Cyrus – Wrecking Ball?

- Look across and realise you are begin interviewed by your ex-partner OR former boss?

- Have every sixth word you say be "stab" OR "Otorhinolaryngologist"?

- Have to perform open heart surgery (you are not a doctor) on your best friend OR defuse a bomb in a puppy Orphanage?

- Only be able to answer questions in the voice of Mr. Burns OR Kermit the Frog?

- Have to tell the interviewer that you once stole their grandma's walking stick OR that you deliberately pushed their child into a pond?

- Have to pick the nose of the interviewer OR pop a spot on their back?

- Shake hands with them after they have just sneezed OR scratched their bare bottom?

More to Come

Phew you survived three years in an underground emergency shelter, avoided the Zombie Koalas and finally decided on the animal legs you have always wanted.

Congratulations on completing this voyage of reflection and self-evaluation. I am sure that you are a far richer and well-rounded person for the experience.

If you have enjoyed this book or feel like you still need further hypothetical therapy watch this space for upcoming titles or check us out at:

Facebook:
https://www.facebook.com/ClintHammerstrike
Website:
www.clinthammerstrike.com
Instagram:
@ClintHammerstrike

Would You Rather Revolution

Check out a sneak peak of another Clint Hammerstrike Masterpiece – Would You Rather Random – Available for purchase on Amazon.

WOULD YOU RATHER:

Take a poo in the toilet of a fancy restaurant and have to wipe up with your underwear OR socks?

WOULD YOU RATHER:

Be hunted by Ninja's or the Mafia?

WOULD YOU RATHER:

Use a koala OR an owl as a towel?

WOULD YOU RATHER:

Lick every object you see OR be licked by everyone that see's you?

WOULD YOU RATHER:

Smell like a skunk OR look like a skunk?

WOULD YOU RATHER:

All the food you ever eat is free OR all the food you ever eat is calorie free?

WOULD YOU RATHER:

Work as a proctologist (anus doctor) OR as a crime scene cleaner?

Work as a whale snot collector (yes its real, and yes it's as disgusting as advertised) OR as a guano collector (fancy term for someone that collects bat and bird poop)?

WOULD YOU RATHER:

Work as a roadkill collector (fox, badger or squirrel get your spade out) OR as an armpit sniffer (how else can deodorant companies know they are doing a good job)?

WOULD YOU RATHER:

Work as an Alaskan crab fisherman (mortality rate 80% higher than average worker, days without showering and 48 hour straight shifts in freezing conditions) OR as a Hurricane Pilot (NASA wants to understand how hurricanes work so they have pilots who fly through them, yup real!)?

WOULD YOU RATHER:

Suffer from Omphalophobia (a fear of the navel) OR Nomophobia (a fear of being without mobile phone coverage)?

WOULD YOU RATHER:

Suffer from Geniophobia (a fear of chins) OR Genuphobia (a fear of knees and/or kneeling)?

WOULD YOU RATHER:

Suffer from Emetophobia (a fear of vomiting) OR Aulophobia (a fear of flutes)?

WOULD YOU RATHER:

Break the record for heaviest weight lifted by an eye socket OR the heaviest weight of bees covering your body?